D1433698

You're Not Going Crazy... You're Just Waking Up!

THE FIVE STAGES OF THE SOUL TRANSFORMATION PROCESS

You're Not Going Crazy...
You're Just Waking Up!

THE FIVE STAGES OF THE SOUL
TRANSFORMATION PROCESS

Michael Mirdad

You're Not Going Crazy...
You're Just Waking Up!

The Five Stages of the Soul Transformation Process

Published by Grail Press

office@GrailProductions.com
www.GrailProductions.com

FOURTH EDITION

Interior and Cover Design by Lanphear Design

Library of Congress Control Number
2008907761

ISBN-13 978-0-9740216-2-1

1.Self-help 2. Spirituality 3. New Age

TABLE OF CONTENTS

ACKNOWLEDGMENTS

The concepts mentioned in this book were developed over many years. They include insights gained from my experiences as a counselor and workshop facilitator, as well as from various studies and personal experiences. Yet, this book would not have been possible were it not for the many clients and friends who successfully went through the Soul Transformation Process and had the courage to speak about their experiences. Many thanks to you all!

My heartfelt thanks to Sally, Jackie, Angela, David, and Gregg for their diligent proofreading and feedback. Also thanks to Robin for her artistic input. Thanks to Lynne Matous for once again sharing outstanding editing skills. I also thank Bob Lanphear for another incredible book design.

Special thanks to Deb and Dan Brown at the Peaceful Heart Center in Michigan. It was while

I was on tour, speaking at their lovely new center, that I received the inspiration to write this book. Miraculously, it then took only a couple of hours to write the first draft and a few days to edit.

Last but not least, I thank God for providing continued healing and inspiration to me and for guiding me to heal and inspire others.

FOREWORD

You're Not Going Crazy . . . You're Just Waking Up! is on the leading edge of a new wave of books designed to help us achieve peace from the inside out as we make our way back to our real Home in Heaven and in perfect oneness with God. *You're Not Going Crazy . . .* shows us all how to create and experience what *A Course in Miracles* refers to as the "Happy Dream."

Michael Mirdad's description of the "five stages of the transformation process," followed by exercises to get us through these stages, is most helpful in alleviating the suffering of some of the more difficult aspects of this process. As a fellow student with a deep understanding of *A Course in Miracles*, Michael Mirdad gives us a highly practical guide (for *ACIM* students and non-students alike) to what one might expect as we begin to experience the process of undoing our egos. Mirdad then lights the way for us as we awaken from our sleep and shift into a new perspective or new life.

Michael Mirdad speaks with a wise voice that helps and inspires us to see that we are not going crazy, nor are we alone, when we go through the various stages of awakening to our true selves. He helps us to see that all of our problems can, and ultimately must, be addressed on a spiritual level, which is the only place where we will find a lasting, and eventually permanent, solution.

Gary Renard, author of the bestseller,
The Disappearance of the Universe

PREFACE

$\mathcal{I}$'ve been a spiritual teacher, healer, and counselor for over 30 years. Whenever people approach me while in a crisis (minor or major), I can't tell you how relieved they feel to hear me explain that what they are going through is a completely "normal" part of the Soul Transformation Process and that all other souls on the planet share this same experience—albeit at different times and in various ways.

Nevertheless, when friends, students, and clients speak or write of their dilemmas, they often begin by saying such things as

+ "I'm so lost."
+ "My life is falling apart."
+ "I'm married, but I'm in love with someone else."
+ "I'm losing my house (job, mind, etc.)."
+ "I'm so confused; I don't know which end is up anymore."
+ "I feel guided to make some changes; but I have it so good, I must be crazy."

All of these statements are symptoms of the same Soul Transformation Process—a process referred to (but practically unnoticed) in the greatest spiritual teachings, such as Buddhism, mysticism, and *A Course in Miracles*. If you've ever been in a similar condition (and who hasn't at some point?), **your soul is beginning to shake things up, question your reality, and guide you to a higher level of consciousness.** To facilitate this transformation, however, your ego-based life first must be Dismantled. A New Life can then be rebuilt on a firmer, more secure foundation—a foundation in Spirit. But, before you can reach the stage of the Soul Transformation Process referred to as "A New Life," you will first feel like you are losing your mind and the life you once knew. It's okay though . . . it's all good!

In other words, "You're not going crazy . . . you're just waking up!"

INTRODUCTION

*H*aving lost sight of its True Nature, every embodied soul goes through a transformational process as a means of awakening, or remembering its Identity. **There are two methods, or paths, by which a soul chooses to "wake up." We either *create a crisis* that brings us to our knees, OR we simply decide that *it makes sense* to move on to a new way of living.** These two options can be defined as learning life's lessons "The *Hard* Way" or "The *Easy* Way."

Learning through rewards is more effective than learning through pain.

—ACIM (A Course in Miracles)

It's going to happen. This unavoidable process, will inevitably surface in your life experience. At some point, your life is going to fall apart, crash, become stagnant or perhaps become unfulfilling. It will happen to you; it will happen to me; it will happen to everyone eventually. It's unavoidable, much like death itself. It's like the old saying, "You can run, but you can't hide." In the pages that follow, this learning experience is referred to as the "Soul Transformation Process."

It is highly advisable not to rush through the reading of this book. Instead, take time to observe the feelings that arise while you are reading and reflect on how this material applies to you and your life.

The Soul Transformation Process can be understood best when divided into its five primary stages: 1) Dismantling, 2) Emptiness, 3) Disorientation, 4) Re-building, and 5) A New Life. These stages usually occur on a daily basis in small ways and/or every few years in larger forms. When these changes occur, the process will manifest as either "The *Easy* Way" or "The *Hard* Way." *You* get to choose which. If you choose to listen to your soul's guidance, your Soul Transformation Process will probably occur the *easy* way. If, however, you don't listen to your soul's guidance, your Soul Transformation Process will probably occur the *hard* way. When manifesting in its most extreme form, the Soul Transformation Process is often referred to as the "dark night of the soul," which is a major life-cleansing process that all people go through at least a few times in their lives.*

The material in this book offers detailed explanations for navigating the curves, bumps, detours, and roadblocks on the proverbial "road of life." But the details of these challenges are only half the story (the part that makes you feel like you are "going crazy") described mostly in the first three stages. The message of this book would not be complete if it did not offer insights into the *purpose*, or end result, of the changes effected by these challenges (the part where you "wake up") described mostly in the last two stages.

An understanding of the Soul Transformation Process and the exercises offered in this book will assist you on your spiritual path. It will not only guide you through the storms, offering daily relief, but also lead you to the "Light at the end of the tunnel," wherein you gain a permanent, new perspective of your life and

---

*More information about the dark night of the soul is available in my book *The Seven Initiations on the Spiritual Path*.

yourself. This new perspective is, of itself, a means for reaching higher levels of spiritual mastery.

After undergoing the Soul Transformation Process and doing some personal and/or spiritual work, you may ask (as have many seekers of Truth): "When will I finally be finished with these lessons (or the Soul Transformation Process)?" The answer is that **when you no longer leave tracks after walking in the mud and no longer cast a shadow while standing in the sun, only then are you done with your lessons.**

Although the Soul Transformation Process is described throughout this book as a five-step process, it could also be described simply as a two-step process: 1) Dismantling (Stages One through Three) and then 2) Rebuilding (Stages Four and Five). It's as though **your psyche is a chalice, or cup, that needs to be *emptied* of old toxic materials so it can be *re-filled* with the fresh waters of life, or new opportunities to live life with more love, peace, and purpose.** In other words, it's letting your "old" self die so that your "new" self can be born.

There is a gap that must be crossed between Stages

Three (Disorientation) and Four (Re-building). If you do not take the "leap of faith" to bridge this gap by learning to surrender, as taught in Stages One through Three, you will simply find a way to recreate your old life by either forcing some pieces back together or recreating a newer version of the *old* life. If upon reaching the Re-building Stage, you draw back or freeze, you will then merely revert to the *first* stage of the Soul Transformation Process—Dismantling. In other words, all you've done is delay the inevitable change that you ultimately need. On the other hand, if you stay on course and move through all of the first three stages properly, you will cross the bridge of faith and progress to Rebuilding a New Life.

---

*The most important thing is this: to be willing
at any moment to sacrifice what we are
for what we can become.*

–Charles Du Bois

THE FIVE STAGES
OF THE SOUL
TRANSFORMATION
PROCESS

THE FIVE STAGES OF THE SOUL TRANSFORMATION PROCESS

*W*hen viewed as a whole, the Soul Transformation Process is like a death and re-birth. Commitment to completing a cycle of this process results in being "born again." This process is meant to cleanse your soul of illusions and unhealthy attachments for the purpose of awakening you to greater realities and to the truth of who you are. **The Soul Transformation Process is aimed predominately at your heart and soul, but it usually becomes evident in either your body (and material life), your emotions (and relationships), and/or your mind (and attitudes).**

There is nothing covered, that shall not be revealed; and hid, that shall not be known.

–Jesus

Your soul has long sought its true nature and its true home—God and Heaven. Since your soul is under the false perception that it is somehow separate from God, it has created what is often called the "soul's journey," which is a journey like all others, a quest to find a treasure or to solve a mystery. In this case, the soul seeks to *learn* and *heal* that which it perceives to be its imperfections. In other words, **the soul focuses on healing any unhealed wounds from the past and/or learning more about its True Identity.**

Maybe the still small voice we are waiting to hear is already in the details of our lives—especially the details we wish would go away and leave us alone.

–Thomas Schmidt, *A Scandalous Beauty*

Some people fear the Soul Transformation Process and all the potential changes it can bring about. Other people welcome it, knowing that they've been putting off making decisions or changes in their lives and NOW is the time to move forward.

Although there are five stages within the Soul Transformation Process, each stage can be viewed as a process unto itself. You will experience these stages in varying degrees and possibly in various orders, but you usually will go through most of the stages, which are as follows:

- **Dismantling**: Here the process begins. You'll either ride along as a participant or you'll get dragged along. Either way, the process starts when there is something about your life that has been stuck or stagnant for too long and is now ready for change. For the addict, this point is reaching bottom. For people who pride themselves on their beauty, money or relationships, it may be learning the hard way that such earthly treasures are worth very little to the soul.

+ **Emptiness**: Now that the illusions you held about your life have been exposed and have begun to dissipate or Dismantle, you'll feel Empty and depressed—mainly due to the time, effort, and (what you thought was) love you've invested in the dissipating illusions. This stage could be seen as a psychological "hang-over" after being drunk on deceptions involving self and others.

+ **Disorientation**: Since the life you thought was intact, needless to say, clearly wasn't, you will now be in a state of Disorientation and possibly doubt everything, including your abilities to do anything right or to make good decisions. Such self-doubt, however, can teach surrender, which is an essential characteristic of a healthy soul.

+ **Re-building**: Now that you seem to have lost something (or maybe everything), you may have learned how to trust and surrender. In so doing, you are probably open to new ideas and inspiration, all of which are leading you to the potential of creating A New Life.

+ **A New Life:** This is the stage wherein you reap the obvious fruits of the healing, patience, and humility that you've developed. Here you are not made small, but great; for now you have released your former identity as an ego-centered human being with human achievements and disappointments. Now you see yourself as far more. Having set aside your limited humanness, you can take the understanding of your Divinity to a whole new level.

The five stages of the soul's transformation are a symbolic movement of the soul through each of the five levels of human consciousness (physical, emotional, intellectual, intuitive, and spiritual). These stages, in turn, symbolize a movement through each of the five elements (earth, water, fire, air, and ether). Therefore, the *Dismantling* Stage will mostly affect your physical, material life. The *Emptying* Stage relates mostly to your emotions. The *Disorientation* Stage relates mostly to your mind and intellect. The *Re-building* Stage relates mostly to your heart, soul, and intuitive creativity. Finally, the Stage of creating *A New Life* relates mostly to your Spirit.

The soul has many reasons for activating this transformational process. Generally speaking, it's the soul's way of expressing "tough love," a way of getting a message across that otherwise you are ignoring. Again, this message usually concerns the need to move to a new level of consciousness that is being held back by either some *lesson* you believe you need to learn or *healing* that is yet incomplete. **Nearly all processes of learning and healing that your soul creates and/or experiences result in opportunities to understand and experience greater levels of unconditional love.** Although not often understood, "unconditional love" refers to more than just loving *people*, it includes loving *all conditions*.

Besides having many *reasons* for activating this transformational process, the soul has numerous *means* for making the process manifest. With some people, it comes in the form of a health crisis, a near-death experience or some form of accident. With others it might come as a personal loss, such as a change in living circumstances. Still others might begin the Soul Transformation Process through a relationship crisis or the appearance into their lives of a man or woman who represents the need to wake up to *old wounds* or perhaps to *new possibilities*.

Whatever it is that activates your Soul Transformation Process, there are three states of mind (or consciousness) individuals manifest as they work through this process. Each potential state of mind speaks to the individual's primary, or most consistent, level of consciousness. The first state of mind, *the victim*, is by far the most common because it is the unfortunate state of mind held by most human beings. The second, *the student*, usually manifests in individuals who are on the "spiritual path" or those who have made a clear commitment to changing their lives. The third, *the master*, is held by individuals who have come to realize that they are indeed co-creators of their lives and the world. This third level is usually attained only by those who have "mastered" being a student. All too often the temptation arises for individuals who are actually in the first or second level of consciousness to attempt to force themselves into this latter level, when in fact they have not yet reached the stage of mastery.

Further explanation of these three stages is as follows:

1. *The Victim*—This is the consciousness (or lack of awareness) that many individuals maintain throughout much of the Soul Transformation Process. These folks continually feel dragged through life's upheavals, instead of seeing "problems" as opportunities to awaken healing and responsibility for their own lives. This "victim" attitude keeps them moving through the first three stages of the Soul Transformation Process, rather than advancing to the higher levels of consciousness in Stages Four and Five.

2. *The Student*—At this level, individuals no longer believe they are merely victims. They do their best to participate consciously in the changes that improve their lives, which allows them to cross the "bridge" into Stages Four (Re-building) and Five (A New Life).

3. *The Master*—Individuals who are masters are unique in that they have the spiritual awareness to "*be the soul itself*" that initiates the Soul Transformation Process. Masters usually choose to dismantle whatever

blocks their spiritual paths or whatever appears in their lives that is not Truth. Once masters become proficient in dismantling their personal illusions about life and themselves, such painful illusions become few and far between. Instead, their lives more consistently manifest harmony.

What should you do to cope with the Soul Transformation Process when it enters your life?

- Prepare in advance. Living a well-balanced life wherein you practice responsibility and self-awareness will cause major shifts to occur less often and less dramatically.

- When it strikes, do what you can to relax into the process and not deny, minimize or blame. Observe the natural stages of the Soul Transformation Process—as outlined in this material. Do your best to work through each stage.

- Cultivate supportive friends who will *not* distract you but, instead, will support your process. Let them know you don't need them to "fix" you or to tell you that *their* lives are even worse. You want them just to listen and be supportive.

✦ Whatever stage of the Soul's Transformation Process you may be in, don't be too hard on yourself. Give yourself credit for each moment of courage and each new insight. Also, practice using an "attitude of gratitude." Be responsible enough to look for any lessons or healings that you need to integrate and then practice giving thanks for them. When you prayerfully give thanks, the universe (and your soul) hears it as a message that you have done your work, feel complete, and are ready to move forward to the next stage.

✦ Once the crisis blows over, don't get too self-inflated, as it can swing back around and humble you. Also, don't "wash your hands and move on" too prematurely. Any bits you miss and fail to process will be back, and multiplied. Instead, during this phase, it's wise to listen and observe inwardly. Be on the look-out for either residual stuff that still needs processing *or* inspirations that begin to appear—offering hints of some new direction.

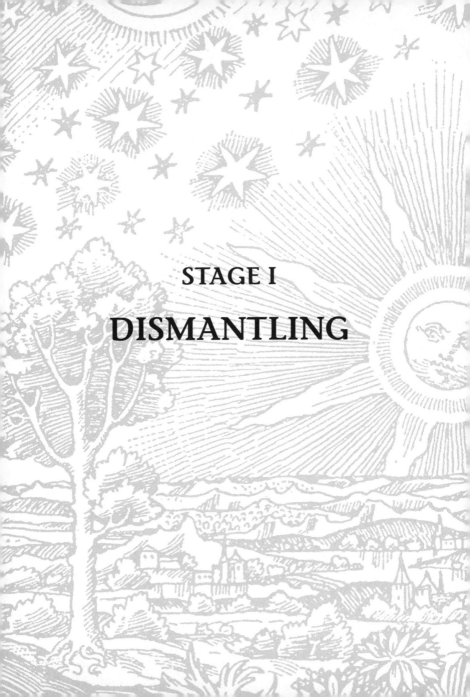

STAGE I

DISMANTLING

DISMANTLING

*H*ere the process begins. You'll either ride along as a participant or you'll get dragged along. Either way, the process starts when there is something about your life that has been stuck or stagnant for too long and is now ready for change. For the addict, this point is reaching bottom. For people who pride themselves on their beauty, money or relationships, it may be learning the *hard* way that such earthly treasures are worth very little to the soul.

People often describe this time in their lives as "falling apart" or "going to pieces" or even "going to hell in a hand basket." What all these colorful metaphors are trying to describe is the natural "Dismantling" of your life as you presently know it.

—————————————•——•——••—————————————

What is happening to me? Crazy some say.
Where is the life that I recognize?

–Duran Duran (Song: "Ordinary World")

—————————————•——•——••—————————————

A Course in Miracles refers to this experience as "a period of undoing." It further states that "This need not be painful, but it usually is. It seems as if things are being taken away, and it is rarely understood initially that their lack of value is merely being recognized . . . and so the plan will sometimes call for changes in what seem to be external circumstances. These changes are always helpful."

The *Course* also defines a secondary aspect to this stage as "a period of sorting out," wherein **you must recognize and accept that some things in your life have simply not truly been valuable or for your highest good.** Seeing this more honestly and clearly will allow you to more easily go through the Dismantling Stage of the Soul Transformation Process.

That which we do not confront in ourselves we will meet as fate. —C. G. Jung

As with all the other phases of transformation, when the Dismantling of your life ensues, you will try to control the stages and outcomes. You will try to rush the process or figure out *where* it's going or *when* it will end. Instead of doing this, you should remain in the present moment—the "here and now." There will be time enough later to deal with the past (during the moments of healing Emptiness, for example) and future (when you receive fresh inspirations for your New Life).

You will also attempt numerous clever (and some not-so-clever) means to "keep it together." You may try minimizing, denying, rationalizing or even quick-fixing, but you would have better luck patching a bursting dam with bubble gum. When your soul says, "enough is enough . . . it's time to make some changes," you'd better take a deep breath and get ready for the ride of your life because things are about to burst open. Believe it or not, it's all for your higher good.

The Dismantling Stage is so thorough and often long-lasting that it's like an entire process unto itself. **The Dismantling Stage can happen—is happening —on many levels and in many dimensions of your life.** Sometimes, on the outside, your life may seem relatively fine. *Internally*, however, you possibly are being "Dismantled." If this is the case, sometimes your *external* life will soon follow and begin to change a little or maybe even fall apart.

At other times, the Dismantling will not manifest or be seen on the outside. Instead, it remains an *internal* process. Nevertheless, you will feel its effects when the Soul Transformation Process reaches the Emptiness Stage. If this is the case, you may, for no reason, begin to feel all the symptoms of going through the Emptiness Stage even without any *tangible* evidence of Dismantling. You may suddenly feel empty, perhaps depressed or tearful, but for no apparent reason.

It's possible that, like most people when their lives are being Dismantled, you will desperately reach for *anything* to console yourself, but nothing will "save" you now from the effects of a much-needed transformation. Gone is the structure that seemed to hold your life together.

Once this process begins, there's really no going back. You can't un-ring the bell or push the snooze button on the "alarm clock of the soul" that's saying it's time to wake up—albeit you will try. The process has begun, and you'll have to ride it out—the *easy* way or the *hard* way. You can reach for any of your old, addictive coping mechanisms (for example: books, money, friends or even some form of fundamental religion). But these can't help you now. Thank God! In fact, outside sources of input may now only make matters worse by distracting your process of healing.

During the Dismantling Stage, some folks even try religiosity. They may say, "If I am a Buddhist or Christian, then shouldn't I be immune to these processes, especially given that Buddha or Jesus already dispelled the powers this world has over me?" Well (despite the noble attempt of offering a good debate), such masters as Buddha or Jesus also taught that although it is their vision for you to accomplish the very level of consciousness *they* had reached, you could do so only by *living* and *maintaining* their particular level of consciousness as you go through life's tests and initiations. Furthermore, the fact that such masters have indeed attained liberated consciousness means that they *can* extend their level of awareness as a gift to you to make your process *easier* but *not* to make your process avoidable.

Since you cannot learn unconditional love for people and things while you are enmeshed with them, many of the people and things to which you are most attached are inevitably taken away. This seeming loss forces you to learn how to let go of unhealthy attachments and develop a greater love that is unconditional. If you are attached to your car, it may get smashed. If you are attached to your home, your mortgage may be foreclosed. Someone may take away your partner. Whatever the case, many (or all) of the things that you thought you "possessed" and formerly depended upon are either gone or no longer work to alleviate the trials of your soul.

Most people try to avoid the chaotic moments that can result from such major changes inherent in the transitional stages of spiritual growth. If they manage to postpone changing, it will only necessitate a larger shift at a later date. Examples of trying to ignore needed changes are numerous. Imagine a man who has a health crisis from working in an unfulfilling job but allows himself to be talked into going right back to work immediate afterwards to fulfill his financial obligations. Did he really do the "right thing?" Or imagine a woman who remains married to an abusive man because she thinks he will reform or because she believes she's too old to attract anyone else or perhaps "for the sake of the kids." In such scenarios, is she really doing the "right thing" by staying?

Your soul knows when you are living in conflict (in body or mind) and are not pursuing your higher good. **Your soul will do something (eventually anything) to wake you up and get you back "on track."** It usually starts with soft, gentle whispers, "Pssst…wake up, Dear One. It's time to alter or release the bad dream you've been having (or living) and wake-up to A New Life." Of course if that doesn't work, the soul may say, "Hey, You! Get up and move your ass, and don't look back!"

Tolerance for pain may be high, but it is not without limit. Eventually everyone begins to recognize, however dimly, that there must be a better way. As this recognition becomes more firmly established, it becomes a turning point.

–ACIM

You may feel as though you are going crazy, having a meltdown, or even having anxiety attacks—all of which can make you feel as if you won't "survive." Nevertheless, you can and will survive the process if you'll just allow yourself to trust and recognize what's really going on … **You are NOT going crazy … You *were* crazy and are now finally becoming sane. You were asleep, and now you are waking up!**

When you are reaching for sanity, one of the "real" problems you will face is that the world and most of its inhabitants are crazy. By making you feel as though it's *you* who has the problem, they are hoping you will rejoin them in their insanity. But, fear not! **It is your destiny to "thaw out" from the numb life you've been living and discover your soul's purpose.** In fact, all the other folks who remain temporarily insane will one day join you in this courageous journey of self-discovery. They, however, will choose *when* that time comes for them. In the meantime, it's possible to use the negative voices of others as tools for growth by realizing that they actually are mirroring your own (sometimes hidden) self-doubts and inhibitions.

You may lose the support of a few friends or family members during the Dismantling process. This possibility may add to your difficulties, but stay the course! **Spirit will see you through and possibly transform friends and family or bring you new friends and family who mirror your *healed* self.**

When a change in relationship does occur, it can be heart-breaking. To be specific, it's more heartbreaking for a woman (because women are more heart-centered). For men, however, such a loss is more mind-breaking (because they are more mind-based). Men usually try to wrap their minds around such losses only to find themselves broken and dumbfounded.

It's also entirely possible that you won't necessarily "lose" people in your life. Instead, the form of the relationship may simply change. Yes, you might lose a relationship, but you might just simply end up nurturing and improving the one you already have.

The emotions that dominate your consciousness during this phase of your life are so intense, you may feel as though a major part of you is dying—and it is. It's a part that you truly want to let die—or let go of—even though you may not always realize this consciously. So, be careful, as you may further complicate the process by clinging to that which is trying to die.

Whosoever shall seek to save his [old] *life*
shall lose it [his New Life].

–Jesus

A most helpful prayer to contemplate during this stage is "Father-Mother God, it looks as though my life is falling apart (or that I am losing such and such), but how would you have me see this?" After praying, be quiet for a moment to let *Spirit's* Reality download into your heart and soul. A response may show up right away, possibly as a sense of peace; or it may appear days later when you simply feel a little less stressed or perhaps feel a profound burst of renewal.

A sure sign of becoming a more responsible, spiritual human being is that you move from being dismantled by forces that seem to be "outside" of you—thus making you feel like a victim—to becoming a "conscious participant" in the Dismantling Stage. The best way to progress to this higher level of consciousness is by going with the flow of (rather than resisting) the Soul Transformation Process and accepting your responsibility to practice the prayers and exercises that can help get you through this period.

Additionally, you can go through this process with an even greater degree of consciousness, personal mastery by learning to actively use the Dismantling Stage as a tool for your higher good. For example, you can choose to bring about an end to something that is not working in your life or perhaps initiate a change in a situation that feels stuck or blocked. In either case, it takes a great deal of courage and trust to participate in Dismantling your own life. It's not unlike a surgeon doing surgery on himself.

To consciously activate the Dismantling Process in your own life, you must first muster up the courage to recognize that something is wrong or missing, much like the child in the fairytale who spoke up and announced, "The emperor is naked." Then, you must become skilled in discerning what is (and isn't) for your higher good, while searching for ways to appropriately release what you no longer truly need—or at least what you are ready to let go of. Fortunately, **if you happen to *miss* something that needs letting go of, your soul will find a way to dismantle it without your conscious choice.**

If, for example, you see that your relationship lacks communication, you need to accept that this situation will not correct itself. If you and your partner do not get help, you can very well assume that your soul will covertly arrange some kind of "shake-up." If you are lucky, this "wake-up call" will manifest in a progressive form of couple's counseling. If you are not so lucky, then either you or your partner could end up with an illness or in an accident. It's also not uncommon for a couple to create such a crisis as one of them having an affair. Of course these are all dramatic examples, but all too often, drama is exactly what people need as their "wake-up call." When you confront your Soul Transformation Process with a higher level of consciousness and responsibility, you will cease waiting for such dramas to occur. Instead, you will take the initiative to Dismantle your problem(s) yourself and make a change in the relationship—one way or another.

As you awaken to your higher good, you will discover how you can also use the Dismantling Stage to your advantage as a tool for peeling away your personal masks and any masks you may have placed over the souls of others.

Most people develop "personality masks" throughout their lives to deal with (or cover up) such core issues as inadequacy or low self-esteem. These masks may be conscious displays of wit, intelligence, good looks, success or any other "crutch" that *seems* to compensate for what they perceive as missing and makes them feel accomplished and more complete.

You may also have less "positive" masks or labels such as being "unlovable," or being "*just* a single parent" or even a "drunk." Whatever the case, a problem remains that if you heal and no longer identify yourself with the personality masks you previously used to hide, survive, and compensate, then who are you?

You might actually panic attempting to "fill in" the blank and end up feeling *Empty* and eventually *Disoriented*. Nevertheless, it's best not to answer this question stemming from your identity crises other than by saying, "I don't know who or what I am, but I'm willing to find out." Then ask God to show you.

Removing such masks creates a "raw" sense of self and often makes you afraid that others will see the wounded part of you that was hiding. The loss of such masks during the Dismantling Stage, therefore, can make you feel vulnerable beyond belief—leading to the next state of the Soul Transformation Process, which is Emptiness.

EXERCISE

Although, for the most part, you should refrain from stepping in and trying to "control" things during the Dismantling Stage, it is sometimes advisable to use this time to take an inventory of yourself and your life. Sit back and take an objective look at what you might do to assist (not resist) the Dismantling Stage. Release old, unneeded things (material possessions) from your life. Similar to a personal version of the ancient art of Feng Shui, keep an open flow of energy in your life by preventing or eliminating both mental and material clutter. Make a list of things you no longer need and then create a specific plan to get rid of those items or pass them on to people who can use them. You'll be surprised at how this simple act of giving not only brings good karma but also alleviates the universe's need to force you to release and thereby brings a faster closure to the Dismantling Stage.

Dismantling Prayer

Father-Mother God, it appears and feels as though my life is falling apart (or that I am losing such and such). Show me how You would have me see and experience this situation. Let me see it through Your eyes and feel it through Your heart.

• NOTES •

STAGE II

EMPTINESS

EMPTINESS

Now that the illusions you held about your life have been exposed and have begun to dissipate or Dismantle, you may feel Empty and depressed—mainly due to the time, effort, and (what you thought was) love you've invested in your illusions. This stage could be seen as a psychological "hang-over" after being drunk on deceptions involving self and others.

When your illusions clash with reality,
when your falsehoods clash with the truth,
then you have suffering.

–Anthony DeMello

After you experience a Dismantling of your life, the next natural stage you go through is Emptiness.

During this stage, you are in a state of either shock or depression or both. Feeling this depth of Emptiness usually upsets your stomach, digestion or appetite and throws your usual life-rhythm way off. The idea of doing anything just for yourself (including the personal enhancement of reading or exercising) may seem like a foreign concept. Your heart and head may hurt, but that's because they are both cracking open for needed healing. You will usually feel lifeless and perhaps want to run away or curl up and disappear.

You may find yourself often thinking or saying the words, "Why bother?" You may even lose the will to live. Remember, this is all just an "ego-tantrum." **Your ego has convinced you that you are *it*, and that *it* is *you*.** Therefore, because a part of *it* (your ego) is dying, you will actually feel as though a part of *you* is dying. Have no fear. Choose to embrace the truth: **A dark part of you and your past is passing away, but *you* can never die.** Know that you are an eternal light—a spark from a yet greater Light.

Drenched by the rains of misfortune, I nevertheless
direct my mind to look always toward thee.
–Paramahansa Yogananda

The truth of the matter is that when your soul activated a Dismantling in your life, it brought up old, unhealed feelings that had been residing (but ignored) deep inside you all along. Much as you might argue to the contrary, the Emptiness you feel now is not solely from your current loss or shift. **You are also feeling the issues of loss and Emptiness from years ago, childhood, and even from the original (seeming) separation from God.** Additionally, you are grieving for your old, familiar identity that is now passing away. And much like a "cat with nine lives," you may find that this death and rebirth happens numerous times in your life.

The stage of Emptiness feels as though you are being crucified, and in a sense you are. The world seems to be killing or crucifying some part of your life. You are dying to the "old self" to make room for the "new self" to be born or resurrected. Seize the moment! Grab hold of this opportunity to deal with the darkest parts of your being while they are exposed. Otherwise, they will descend back into the hidden recesses of your mind and become like "ghosts" that cry out for attention and healing. Furthermore, much like computer viruses, they will corrupt many of the new, healthier programs you attempt to implement into your life. Don't be afraid to look at this old, dark "programming" to aid in its releasing and passing. After all, even Jesus himself is said to have descended into hell for three days before ascending into Heaven.

During the Emptiness Stage, you hopefully will shed a lot of cleansing tears because the ones you fail to release now will be "knocking at the door" of your tear ducts tomorrow. **The tears of the soul fall hard and/or continuously.** Then, just when you think you're done crying, there's more—so much more. Nevertheless, if you *do* finally reach a state of "completion" wherein you have cleared the old tears from the fountains of your soul, you'll probably enter a new level of mourning. Now you'll begin crying tears for the wounds of *all souls* for *all time*. You'll access the woundedness held within the collective unconscious of all beings. It may seem an insurmountable task, but in truth, it's your destiny to accomplish this and all other spiritual initiations. In fact, by doing your part to "survive" this experience, you will ease the burden of others who follow, just as others have eased the burden you now carry—even if at times it doesn't feel that way.

The Emptiness Stage usually brings up issues of mortality. You may contemplate your inevitable death (or perhaps think of taking your own life). Whichever the case, much like a person who is growing old in years, you may find yourself going for a walk down "memory lane." During this stage, it's normal to literally or mentally visit your home of birth, your old school, old friends, or perhaps listen to music that evokes memories—happy or sad.

What you *should* do, during the stage of Emptiness, is the exact opposite of what most people *choose* to do, which is, "Be with it." In other words, hang in there and observe the deeper, older significance of these feelings and the process itself. Remember, "This too shall pass." **If you choose to relax into the Emptiness, it can actually turn into a deeply peaceful place where you rest from the recent upheavals.** Furthermore, "relaxing into an experience" is far more beneficial than it may seem. It's more than merely making things easier. The very act itself gives you new-found discipline, a gift that later will serve you well in ways beyond your present imagining.

There is a story of a farmer who has a large fruit tree blown over by strong winds. His neighbor shouts across the field to him, expressing his condolences for the loss of such a great fruit tree. He also asks the farmer if he's now going to chop up or burn the tree. The farmer replies that he will indeed burn the tree but only *after* he removes all of the valuable fruit. The moral of the story is that you should **learn to extract the valuable lessons held within each experience**

(however seemingly negative) before you try to destroy the memory.

Again, you may attempt to deal with either the Dismantling or Emptiness by grabbing hold of some *person* or some *thing* to try to fill the void you feel inside. It may even seem that the void is *outside*—like missing a body to hold—but in reality, it's always about a deeper void on the *inside*. Ironically, if you keep the faith through these moments of despair, you eventually discover that the void of darkness that once seemed to smother and engulf you now becomes a peaceful silence, or stillness. Although the feeling may be fleeting, it is nonetheless refreshing.

A Course in Miracles refers to this relaxing as a *"period of settling down . . . a quiet time, wherein you can rest awhile in reasonable peace."* It further advises that *"You have not come as far as you think. Yet,* [after the rest in Emptiness] *when you are ready to go on, you will do so with mighty companions beside you."*

Blessed are they that mourn:
for they shall be comforted.

–Jesus

Similar to all of your spiritual brothers and sisters before you who have endured the Soul Transformation Process, you will be tempted to doubt the very existence of God or wonder how or why "He" could let this happen to you. You might find yourself crying out to God, "*Take this cup* [problem] *from me.*" Rather, try saying, "God, although I am afraid and long to have this experience taken from me, I ask instead that you be with me *while* I go through it." This is similar to the biblical saying, "*Yea, though I walk through the valley of the shadow of death, I will fear no evil: for Thou art with me.*"

I know God will not give me anything I can't
handle. I just wish that He didn't trust me so much.

–Mother Teresa

There are several common mistakes that many people make during the Emptiness Stage. These mistakes may include any of the following: 1) Coping with feeling Empty (or being Dismantled, for that matter) by remaining in denial and refusing to make any changes or adjustments to their thoughts, attitudes, beliefs or behaviors; 2) Being too stubborn to reach out for help from safe people or healthy support systems (As the book of Proverbs says, *"Pride cometh before a fall"*); and 3) Choosing to remain stuck either in the pain of being Dismantled or the ensuing feeling of Emptiness. People who knowingly or unknowingly choose any of these unfortunate options, may find themselves cycling around and around the Dismantling and Emptiness Stages without moving forward into the next stage, Disorientation, which acts as a bridge to the end of suffering.

EXERCISE

Whenever you experience Emptiness (or any of its symptoms, such as depression or loneliness), use the following basic "tracking exercise."

1. Repeat the following to yourself, "I recognize that I am feeling (insert the emotion, such as 'sad,' 'alone,' etc.)."

2. Then repeat, "I accept that there are other times in my life when I similarly have felt this way, such as (spontaneously fill in the blank with the most dominant memory of a person or incident in your life that also brought up this emotion)." Chances are, the past event that comes up was never healed to completion and is adding to or causing your current emotional crisis.

3. Prayerfully offer this old wound (or wounds), as well as the current crisis, to Spirit/God.

4. Choose now to call something new into your heart

and soul. Do this by calling light into your heart-center, as you draw in deep, relaxing breaths. While visualizing this light entering your being, imprint it with a word or two of your choice (such as "love," "peace" or "joy").

5. Give thanks!

Emptiness Prayer

My Father-Mother God, although I feel afraid and long to have this experience taken from me, I ask instead that you be with me while I go through this. In so doing, I know together we will transform the experience and all the beliefs that brought it about, thus leading me to A New Life.

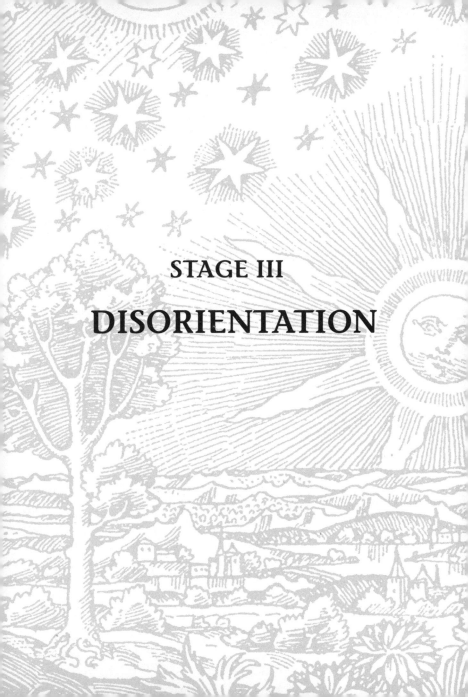

STAGE III

DISORIENTATION

DISORIENTATION

Needless to say, since the life you thought was intact, clearly wasn't, you will now be in a state of Disorientation and possibly doubt everything, including your abilities to do anything right or to make good decisions. Such self-doubt however, can teach surrender, which is an essential characteristic of a healthy soul.

The state of being, or feeling, Disoriented sometimes hits *before* the Emptiness Stage but usually follows it. Although the *Emptiness Stage* (which purges you *emotionally*) can cause you to feel *depressed*, **the Disorientation Stage cleanses you *mentally*, stripping away the thought processes you once clung to and most likely leaving you with *self-doubt*.** In fact, you might feel as though you trust neither yourself nor others.

After going through some Dismantling and then feelings of Emptiness (at times gut-wrenching Emptiness), you may begin to feel Disoriented. This is to be expected given that you are used to feeling somewhat more "in control" of your life and surroundings. Needless to say, **the more you are attached to controlling your life and the lives of others around you, the more you will feel Disoriented when such control is gone.**

During this Disorientation Stage (and the previous two stages), one of the most confusing lessons you encounter involves knowing when to "fight back" or when to "surrender to the process." Indeed, there are times wherein your "lesson" is about standing up for what you believe. Still other times the lesson is about expressing your need to practice being a co-creator and working a little harder to "manifest the life you want." But there are also times when the universe is telling you to let go and stop fighting the situation. Even when confronted with disease and death itself, there are times when it's best to fight for your life; but it's just as possible that it may be a time to surrender and walk on through the doorway of Light.

There is no way to always know for sure which path you should take. There is, however, one wise, general rule to follow: If, and/or when, you have done all you can to make something happen, but you're still at a dead-end, it's possibly a sign that you need to back off and stop forcing the issue. This principle is not unlike the concept of God resting for a day after the first six days, or periods, of creation. Furthermore, as stated in Ecclesiastes, *"To every thing there is a season, and a time to every purpose under the heaven."*

Your old ego-based mind will be in a panic because it knows that when *you* surrender control of your life, *it* loses control of your life. So it will say something like, "It's about time you stopped obsessing on this idea of 'improving your life.' Now get up and let's get back to 'our' old (miserable) life." But when you look around, nothing seems or feels the same. That's because nothing *is* the same. Of course at this point, your ego-mind will go into a panic and cry out, "Look what you've done!" It then tries to convince you to re-create your old, familiar life. **The ego-mind needs things to be familiar because it has spent years getting you stuck here in the first place.**

The Disorientation Stage is not only a psychological state of being but also usually manifests in your day-to-day life. You might get into your car and forget where the key goes; you might walk into a room and forget why you went in there; perhaps you dial a number and forget *who* you called or *why* you called. Yes, of course, this can happen to anyone who is momentarily distracted; but during the Soul Transformation Process, the cause is quite different and has much deeper implications. As in the stages of Dismantling and Emptiness, you may long for control, which makes sense given that once you begin to feel Disoriented, you also feel "out of control" and therefore seek to manage this situation by trying to regain control.

The problem is that if we regain control, we've put our *ego-based minds* in the seat of power, rather than our *soul-based hearts*. The concept of letting the (God-focused) heart become our guide may seem foreign and frightening to some. This is especially true if we are convinced that the mind is the "problem solver" —which is what we think we need when we are in crisis.

A Course in Miracles refers to the Disorientation Stage as *"a period of unsettling . . . Now must you understand that you did not really know what was* [truly] *valuable and what was valueless. And now you must learn to lay all judgment aside, and ask only what you really want in every circumstance."*

Disorientation usually begins in an area that you feel is important—where you have attachments or where your pride resides—so you will take notice. Instead of panicking or "getting down" on yourself for feeling less alert or not "having it all together," try to recognize this stage for what it is and laugh. Say to yourself, "Ohhhhh, that's right . . . I'm not going crazy after all. I'm just 'Disoriented' because my life and illusions are falling apart."

Doubt along the way will come and go and go and come again . . . When you forget, remember that you walk with Him and with His Word upon your heart. —ACIM

This stage involves letting go of a fear-based life and your old perceptions. It's about learning to surrender to a Higher Power that may have seemed far away or even non-existent but now is drawn closer by your choice to surrender. **During the Disorientation Stage, you learn lessons in surrender and unconditional love, which means letting go of some of the tools and coping-skills you formerly relied upon.**

Just as it was possible to experience the Emptiness Stage without recognizing that you went through the Dismantling Stage, it's possible to experience the Disorientation Stage without noticing either of these previous two stages. You may simply start feeling Disoriented but feel uncertain as to why. If this occurs, you could very well have passed through the other stages on a subconscious level—or even a conscious level but without paying them much attention. If you experience a feeling of inexplicable Disorientation, it would be wise to do a self-inventory and look to see what you may have missed and can now learn retro-actively. If you cannot discover any trace of having been through the other stages, then simply direct your attention to where you are now and follow the advice given for this Disorientation Stage.

To assist in the process of learning to let go and surrender, repeat to yourself: "I don't understand anything, nor do I know what anything is for." Although this statement may sound self-depreciating, it acknowledges that you are *vulnerable* and don't know as much as you once thought you knew—which becomes more obvious with every heartbreaking moment of the Soul Transformation Process.

Acknowledging that you don't know or understand anything (which is often referred to as having a "beginner's mind" or "being as a child") may feel difficult at first. Yet if you honestly observe your life, you will indeed realize that you have not been *experiencing* the people and objects in your life as they *truly* are. Instead, your view of everyone and everything has been biased—seen through the filters of your own past experiences and perceptions.

Once you reach this stage of the Soul Transformation Process, there is no doubt you are changing the way you choose to see or experience people and even life itself. Such commitment inevitably takes you to a new, much higher level of consciousness.

Now, even if it seems as though it took a lifetime, the storm is "blowing over." You have endured a major, life-changing process, and you will never be the same. It's time to come back to life and start again. It's time to begin Re-building your life. This time, however, if you've learned anything from the recent experiences and have developed a healthy level of surrender, your new life will be built with (and from) much greater love and inspiration. On the other hand, **if your fears and controlling behaviors get the best of you, you'll probably end up back at the First Stage of the Soul Transformation Process, and being Dismantled—yet again.**

EXERCISE

If you notice that you are experiencing a moment of Disorientation, center yourself by taking a couple of deep, relaxing breaths. Then remind yourself of the following: "I recognize that I'm feeling Disoriented. I know that this is because something inside of me is coming to the surface and (on some level) I must be feeling afraid. The cause of whatever I am feeling or experiencing (which is causing me to panic and become Disoriented) is *not* happening right now. It is something from the past that is surfacing to be healed. I choose to surrender whatever this is to you, my Father-Mother God, and also choose to have it replaced by your Holy Presence."

Disorientation Prayer

God leads me and knows the way, which is currently obscured to me. At this time, I don't truly understand anything I see or anything I am experiencing. But I know that hidden behind the veil of illusion lies my True Life and my True Identity, and so I now surrender to this Reality—God's Reality.

• NOTES •

STAGE IV

RE-BUILDING

RE-BUILDING

$\mathcal{N}$ow that you seem to have lost something (possibly everything), hopefully you've learned how to trust and surrender. In so doing, you probably are open to new ideas and inspirations, all of which are leading you to the potential of creating A New Life.

Ever since the Dismantling Stage originally began, you were probably trying to regain control and attempting to Re-build your life, but your attempts at that point would have been far too premature.

In case you hadn't noticed, human beings tend to be control-freaks. **The propensity to "jump in" and take control is *never* stronger than when you feel afraid and/or out of control.** Nevertheless, do what you can to refrain from jumping in and meddling with things. As much as you can, and as often as possible, let go of the desire to control. As *A Course in Miracles* expresses it, "*A healed mind does not plan . . . [but it] . . . carries out the plans that it receives through listening to wisdom that is not its own.*" Allow Spirit to guide you, and you'll discover a spiritual power within that's far greater than any of your control tactics. You are about to "turn the corner" and enter into A New Life, but it must be a life not built with human minds or hands. Again, instead of trying to take control, wait! **Be still and allow God to inspire your new direction and the next steps you should take.**

Remember, your New Life may not look the same as the old one, but in the end, all will be well. **Your life *will* be far better than before the Soul Transformation Process began—that is, as long as you stay out of the way.** There is no doubt that once the "fallout" from this process settles, the level of consciousness you emerge with will be contingent upon what you did and how you handled yourself *during* the process.

Now that you've been through varying degrees of hell, you realize that life is not about trying to control your own destiny and then sending out superstitious cries to an invisible deity when you hit a snag or rough spot. In other words, **to *know* God, you must be *as* God.** In essence, the first step to actualizing this renewal of your soul is to "get out of the way". The second step is to bring God into every aspect of your being, so you can become more *like* God. Therefore, do and think only what your heart and soul tells you God would do and think.

Religion is for people who fear hell, but spirituality is for those who have been there!

–Unknown

A Course in Miracles refers to the Re-building Stage as a *"period of achievement."* Furthermore, it says that *"what was seen as merely shadows before, becomes solid gains to be counted on in all emergencies as well as tranquil times."* One of the "solid gains" most frequently achieved includes glimpses into your true destiny or soul's purpose. Although everyone has some sort of a *future*, not everyone will choose to fill that future with *purpose*.

At the Re-building Stage, you begin to see the light at the end of the tunnel. Don't run! Just walk. **This is a time for rejuvenating, receiving guidance for your next steps, and implementing those new ideas and inspirations.** So be open to inspiration. Open your heart as fully as possible to allow Spirit to fill the *healthy* version of Emptiness you now feel. As *A Course in Miracles* advises, *"Make it a habit to ask for help where and when you can; you can be confident that all wisdom will be given when you need it."* Also, spend more time praying, meditating, and affirming Truth.

Now that you've emptied the old contents of your cup (consciousness), God will refill it (you) with new understanding. **If you want something new in your life, it's necessary to set aside previous learning and experiences that conflict with the new awareness of who you truly are.** Otherwise, you will invariably revert to former beliefs and experiences to define yourself.

Even though you may have increased your understanding that this world is primarily an illusion, while you are here and believe in the illusion, it can be put to good use. Practice bringing God (Peace and Love) into every part of this illusionary world, if only one illusion at a time. In so doing, you are actually expanding Heaven. **You don't need to fight or resist illusions, merely allow them to gently be replaced by new perceptions.**

A *Course in Miracles* explains that generally the use of denial is an unhealthy and unproductive tactic. However, it does promote ONE use of denial, and that is as follows: When you choose to give up an old pattern or belief-system, you are encouraged also to prayerfully give up the karmic effects of that previous pattern. Be sure to stand in your courage and say, "I release all limiting former beliefs about who I am and what I deserve in my life, *and* I deny the effects of those previous decisions." This affirmation should be followed by, "Instead, I now choose to allow God to decide who I am and what I deserve when I align myself with my Higher Good [also known as 'God's Will']. I also choose to receive the natural, loving gifts that come with making this healthy, new choice."

While your life was in transition and it seemed you might lose (or did lose) much of what you believed was important for your happiness, you couldn't imagine a better life—one with a greater good. Now is your chance to begin seeing glimpses of that new potential—A New Life. If you didn't like your former life, that's great because now you can build one that's more to your liking. On the other hand, if you *did* like your life, that's great too because now you can build an even better one. Believe it!

There are several things you can do to nurture the Re-building Stage. Two of the most important things to remember are as follows: 1) Think and speak only positive words, doing away with mental and verbal negativity. This includes the narcissistic tendency to make all conversations revolve around you. 2) Learn to deal with thoughts and fears the way a warrior deals with going into battle or the way a spiritual master seeks to deal with any challenge—"divide and conquer." Make it a habit to confront and analyze any issues or unhealthy patterns that arise in your life. Look at them head-on and dismantle them and their power by asking such questions as, "Is this problem as real and present as I believe it to be?" Or, "Is my reaction coming from love or fear?" Or, "If the worst case scenario actually happened, what am I *really* afraid of?" Such courage and clarity are what it takes for true co-creators to see the fruits of the New Life awaiting them in the next stage.

EXERCISE

The following is perhaps the most effective exercise to assist the Re-building process. It is similar to what many shamans refer to as "dreaming the world into being." It's best to practice each morning and evening, when you first wake up and before sleep, as follows:

1. As you inhale deeply, imagine drawing light down into your heart-center from the heavens (symbolizing God). Simultaneously, concentrate on the words "love and self-worth" (or any other word or words that most depict the state of consciousness you desire). In so doing, you are programming your heart and soul with these new patterns. After anchoring these traits (via words and feelings) into your heart-center, exhale slowly as you allow the light to spread from your heart-center to every cell of your body, bathing you completely. As you do this, allow yourself to hear the words "And so it is." Then repeat this process approximately a dozen times and proceed to step two.

2. Spend at least 5-10 minutes visualizing and *feeling* your life as you would like it to be. Look at each major category of your life (such as health, finances, relationships, and work). Ask yourself, "If I am indeed filled with 'love and self-worth' (or whatever words you've chosen), what would my life look and feel like (in each of these major categories)?" Then respond by visualizing and feeling the answer in a living form, as though it's

already happening—right now. For example, if you were to choose to see yourself healthy, you might visualize and feel yourself exercising in a form that you enjoy (perhaps yoga). See yourself doing the yoga postures and feeling the effects in your body. This might include seeing and feeling your joints being more open and your body less stiff or sore.

3. Always close such exercises by giving thanks in advance that anything you just imagined, while attuned to Spirit and aligned with your highest good, is already being brought into manifestation.

Re-building Prayer

My Father-Mother God, fill my heart, mind, soul, and body with Your perfect and Holy Presence. Show me what you would have me do today and where you would have me go, as well as what you would have me say and to whom.

• NOTES •

STAGE V

A NEW LIFE

A NEW LIFE

*T*his is the stage wherein you reap the obvious fruits of the healing, patience, and humility you've developed. Here you are not made small, but great; for **now you have released your former identity as an ego-centered human being with human achievements and disappointments. Now you see yourself as far more.** Having set aside your limited humanness, you can take the understanding of your Divinity to a whole new level.

In the previous stage of Re-building, you received new inspirations and hopefully implemented these new ideas. Now, in this stage of "ANew Life," you begin to *see, feel,* and *experience* the *effects* of your new ideas (or fruits of your labors).

In *A Course in Miracles*, it states that this is a *"stage of real peace, for here is Heaven's state fully reflected. From here, the way to Heaven is open and easy."*

You may assume that once you have "completed" the Soul Transformation Process, you need not go through it again. But, no such luck! While in a body, you always will experience the Soul Transformation Process to some degree. However, you increasingly learn to "allow" the process and "go with the flow," *and* with less resistance. As your consciousness evolves to a higher level of awareness, the transformational process often is less dramatic. **In your higher awareness, you have fewer attachments and obstacles to being unconditional in your love, which means less healing and fewer lessons needed.** The Soul Transformation Process may still be experienced, but it will not reflect lessons of pain and loss. Instead, transformation can be simply a spiral-like movement into higher and higher states of consciousness.

Even though you've learned how to plant the seeds of A New Life during the Re-building Stage, it's still essential that you take responsibility to protect and maintain those seeds. You have to water and feed them and see to it that you keep the weeds from killing your New Life.

Another crucial activity during this stage is to share some of the new love, insights, creativity, abundance, compassion or whatever else you've acquired. This is essential advice because **you *keep* only the gifts that you *share* with others.** It doesn't matter with *whom* you share as long as you share. When deciding *how* to share, be careful not to "preach" to others or attempt to give where your gift is not welcome. Instead, be sure to ask for Spiritual Guidance concerning what to share, as well as when and how. You can use the decision-making criteria in the exercises below, simply asking what and when giving will bring the most good to the most people.

EXERCISE 1

Watch carefully to ensure that every decision, action, and word that you choose builds the New

Life of love and self-worth that you are praying for. In other words, your actions and decisions should add to, rather than subtract from, the nurturing of love, peace, joy, and abundance. If your words and actions contribute to your long-term peace and happiness, they probably are the "right" decisions for you. If such actions and decisions conflict with your long-term well being, they're probably *not* "right" for you. To continue building your New Life and a new, healthier self with healthier boundaries, surrender your every thought, word, and action to a Power beyond the laws and logic of this world. If you follow the tangible guidance in your heart that clearly promotes love, rest assured that this is inspiration, or the Voice of God.

EXERCISE 2

One of the most valuable and consistently useable "tools" gained from the Re-building process is that of making healthier choices. An important criteria, or gauge, to use in making these better choices is to ask yourself, "What decision will bring the most love, peace, and joy to the most people—in the long run?" This question will help you in deciding nearly everything from which car to buy and which video to rent, to which person to date. The challenge here is to remember that *you* also are one of those people whose "good" you need to consider. It rarely serves the greater good for you to help others while sacrificing yourself. In fact, it sends out an unhealthy message to everyone that says, "I don't matter." This subliminal message can draw people into your life who will confirm that mistaken belief. Furthermore, it teaches loved ones, like your children, that they too may not matter and should not honor their own needs and boundaries.

New Life Prayer

*I live in constant gratitude for all the
love, peace, joy, and abundance that God
brings to me. The Light of God has come
and fills me with many miracles.
My cup runneth over.*

• NOTES •

CONCLUSION

*H*aving read and hopefully integrated this material, it should be clear that **when you *consciously* engage in the Soul Transformation Process, rather than being *dragged* through it, you progress from being a mere "student of life" to being a "graduate of life's initiations"—shifting from being a "student" to becoming a "living master."** You are now becoming a participant in the co-creation of life. Of course you will still go through the Soul Transformation Process, but the experience is usually briefer and far less painful.

People choose to "get their act together," becoming conscious participants on their paths (or the heroes in their personal mythologies) for one of two reasons: either they hit bottom and are tired of crisis *or* simply because it makes sense to do so. In other words, instead of moving toward the "light at the end of the tunnel" because they are *tired of darkness*, those individuals who choose the latter reason do so because they have learned to *love the light* and all that it offers. To choose the latter means that you have begun to learn life's lessons "the easy way," which is far *less* painful, far *more* inspiring, and saves you a great deal of time and effort.

Whether or not you go through this process with high levels of conscious involvement, you are always a different person when the "dust settles." And if *you* are different, you can bet that your *life* will be different too—just *how* different will depend on how you handled yourself during the Soul Transformation Process. As with everything, the more you put into it, the more you will get back.

And in the end . . . The love you take . . .
Is equal to the love . . . You make . . .
–The Beatles (Song: "The End")

As stated in the Introduction, the purpose of this book is not just to explain *why* your life was in upheaval and *why* you felt as though you were "going crazy." The purpose (and promise) is also to offer insights into the means of "waking up." The prayers and exercises offered throughout this material will indeed connect you to the "Light at the end of the tunnel." **Although you may still have doubts and difficulties in life, you are meant to become a more active participant in the Dismantling of the aspects of your life that fail to resonate with your Highest Good.** Additionally, you are meant to become an active participant in the Re-building of your New Life that does indeed resonate with your Highest Good.

Even though you might never imagine wishing this process onto anyone, in truth, the Soul Transformation Process (and its extreme version known as "the dark night of the soul") is the most powerful initiatory process known to mankind. The pain and discomfort has the potential of giving way to trust, illumination, and an overall healthier life. This process is not unlike childbirth—painful for a while but all that seems to fade away when you look into the eyes of New Life.

In the meantime, you still have to function. You

may have children to tend to, a relationship to deal with, a job to perform, a phone to answer, your body to care for, and so on. **You may want to give up and run away, but you don't have to.** You can set aside time to deal with your day-to-day responsibilities (even if it feels like you're just going through the motions). But also spend some time dealing with your soul's transformation. "Know the truth [you are going through a terrifying shift guided by Spirit], but respect the illusion [you must still deal with your daily responsibilities]." You may wait until evening when things are quiet around the house and spend some time journaling about your shifts in consciousness. Be careful, though. If others read your writings, they may misconstrue your words or use them against you.

While you are going through the dynamics of this shift, it is imperative that you avoid inadvertently becoming an abuser. Although you know this is never your intention, it's not uncommon to neglect aspects of your life, have too many meltdowns in front of the kids, or unleash excessive amounts of your pent up anger onto others. Also avoid acting out your repressed sexual energy with other men or women who enter your life—a means common to both genders for either "venting" or compensating for unhealed hurts and frustrations. Again, men and women differ somewhat emotionally and psychologically. In such cases as these, a woman who is dissatisfied with *her* life is often *romanced* into an affair and away from *her* "center" and self-worth. On the other hand, a man who is dissatisfied with *his* life is often *seduced* into an affair and away from *his* "center" and self-worth.

In either case, the root cause and outcome are the same—unhealed issues leading to losing your centered-self, resulting in hurting yourself and others. Such inadvertent abuse is proof positive that you've become so afraid in your Dismantling, Emptiness and/or Disorientation that you've allowed your ego to gain control. You should indeed "let go and surrender to the process," but you must always maintain your center by remaining a responsible "witness" to the process.

So, in the end, what is it all for? What is the reward for all of your patience and tenacity? In truth (literally and metaphorically), it could be summarized by saying that **you have given up** *nothing* **to gain** *everything.* If you lose *anything* whatsoever, it is *nothing* that serves your Highest Good. And what you gain is what you most need to put you in touch with your True Self and the Spirit of Love that Created you. Thus, on both a daily and long-term basis, you gain *everything* you've ever dreamed of and *everything* your soul has ever longed for. This new perspective (New Life) is described in *A Course in Miracles* as, "*A future undisturbed, without a trace of sorrow, and with joy that constantly increases.*"

And I saw a new heaven and a new earth: for the
first heaven and the first earth were passed away.
–the Bible

• NOTES •

• NOTES •

WORKSHOP INTENSIVES
Offered by Michael Mirdad

There are three primary workshop intensives offered by Michael Mirdad. The first, in the spring, is Healing: Body and Soul and is designed to bring the attendees to new levels of physical, emotional, and spiritual health, while also teaching them how to become healers (or better healers). The second, in the summer, is Living Mastery. This workshop is great for anyone who is ready to discover new levels of direction, responsibility, balance, and wholeness. The third workshop, in the fall, Initiations Into Christ Consciousness, teaches attendees to connect with their True (Christ) Self and deeper levels of spiritual awareness.

HEALING: BODY & SOUL

This workshop is a 5-day intensive for anyone seeking to receive physical and/or emotional healing or choosing to develop greater healing abilities. It is perfect for those wanting to renew their commitment to maintaining physical/emotional health and spiritual connectedness and includes training in herbology, massage, energy work, Tai Chi, acupressure, Reiki, emotional healing, yoga, cranial release and health intuitiveness.

"I am so grateful that the workshop re-ignited or deepened the healer in me. I absolutely loved using a combination of breath work, physical body work, intuition, and advanced techniques to trigger issues on a cellular level to bring them forth to be healed. We learned healing and counseling skills that most counselors don't even know!" –Ron, ONT

LIVING MASTERY INTENSIVE

This workshop is a 5-day intensive for those who are prepared to live a life of fulfillment. It teaches how to experience the best life possible in every aspect of living. No other single event offers so much! Living Mastery is an advanced training for students and teachers of spirituality who are ready to learn how to manifest a spiritual, integrated, balanced, and prosperous life, as well as learning how to bring God and all spiritual learning into their daily lives and activities. Topics include the following: physical mastery—manifesting prosperity, living healthy through yoga and diet, and training in several healing arts; emotional mastery—developing psychic abilities, creating fulfilling relationships, and learning advanced emotional healing techniques; mental mastery—developing greater focus, learning effective meditation, and discovering your soul's purpose; and spiritual mastery—developing a life plan, learning true forgiveness, awakening higher levels of consciousness, and opening your heart center.

"I am so honored to have had the opportunity to experience five of the most amazing days of my life, while attending the Mastery Workshop. I became aware of my strength and endurance through rock climbing, yoga, and the obstacle course. I embraced exercises in past life regression and emotional healing. I was challenged doing exercises in cloud busting and learning the importance of focusing, as well as dividing and conquering life's obstacles. And I learned the importance of prayer and meditation and letting God live through me every instant of my life." —Janet, NY

INITIATIONS INTO
CHRIST CONSCIOUSNESS

This 5-day workshop is an advanced training for students and teachers of Christ Consciousness. It covers advanced teachings and spiritual concepts, as well as profound levels of application. Attendees learn to clear their centers of consciousness and live a life that reflects their higher self in mind, body, and soul. This workshop also covers the following: initiations into Christ Consciousness through rarely understood mystery teachings of Jesus—some of which were transferred to Mary Magdalene, clearing of various energy centers (chakras), the secret teachings of Christ, Jesus' missing years amongst the Essenes and the Mystery Temples, and experiencing your own spiritual baptism.

"There were so many wonderful activities at this workshop. The information about the history of the universe was clear, informative and intriguing. The closing initiation into the Christ Consciousness was transformative. When I lay down in the middle of the circle, I felt the amplification of energy, all the light, in my body. As my heart chakra opened, I felt as if my entire chest were being pulled up to the ceiling, while my breath was deep and being pulled through my body to my feet. I felt like I was in the zone of Jesus, Mary, and of course fellow attendees. I feel as though I have attained a new spiritual level." —Jean, OR

SACRED SITES JOURNEYS

With Michael Mirdad

THE INITIATORY JOURNEY

Since the beginning of time, students and masters on the spiritual path have taken journeys of initiation to sacred sites. These holy places included France, Egypt, Central America, and England. Initiates brought with them a sacred technology to build temples, megaliths, and ascension sites for healing and for harnessing the Earth's grid system.

Today these journeys still serve as a powerful ritual for personal power and spiritual awakening for planet Earth and all its inhabitants. Come and join us in this personal and planetary awakening.

SAMPLES OF SOME OF OUR JOURNEYS

FRANCE
Grotto-Home of Mary Magdalene
St. Marie de La Mer
Lourdes
Sacred Cathar & Templar Sites
France's Mount of St. Michael
IRELAND
Newgrange
Sacred Hill of Tara
Numerous Ancient Goddess Sites
SCOTLAND
Findhorn
Scottish Highlands
Magical Iona Island
Rosslyn Chapel

ENGLAND
Crop Circles
Avebury & Stonehenge
Glastonbury Abbey
The Chalice Well
Numerous Arthurian Sites
GREECE
Delphi
Legendary Islands
Athens
EGYPT
Great Pyramids
Valley of the Kings
Karnak
Temples of the Nile

Price includes: international travel from US and back, shared lodging, tour guides, most meals, entrance to sacred sites, teaching sessions, and more. Space is limited! Contact us now to register or to get on our mailing list.

Grail Productions, PO Box 2783, Bellingham, WA 98227

For information: 360-671-8349 or office@grailproductions.com
Visit us at www.GrailProductions.com

ORDER FORM

To order any of our books or request more information on any of these publications, please copy and mail in this order form or call our office or visit our website for a complete list of books, CDs, and DVDs.

Name_____

Adress_____

City, State, Zip_____

Phone_____

Email_____

Please include any special instructions when ordering.
Make checks payable to: Grail Productions

_____

_____

An Introduction to Tantra and Sacred Sexuality
_____ copies at $15.00 each =   _____

Sacred Sexuality: A Manual for Living Bliss
_____ copies at $25.00 each =   _____

Seven Initiations of the Spiritual Path
_____ copies at $15.00 each =   _____

Healing the Heart & Soul
_____ copies at $15.00 each =   _____

You're Not Going Crazy...You're Just Waking Up!
_____ copies at $15.00 each =   _____

Add $2.50 for S&H per book   _____

Total   _____

Grail Productions, PO Box 2783, Bellingham, WA 98227
For information: (360) 671-8349 or office@grailproductions.com
Visit us at www.GrailProductions.com

About the Author

Michael Mirdad is a world-renowned spiritual teacher, healer, and author. He has worked as a healer and counselor for over 30 years and is the author of the best-selling books *The Seven Initiations of the Spiritual Path, An Introduction to Tantra and Sacred Sexuality,* and *Healing the Heart & Soul.* Michael has facilitated thousands of classes, lectures, and workshops throughout the world on Mastery, Spirituality, Relationships, and Healing and is commonly referred to as a "teacher's teacher" and a "healer's healer."

Michael Mirdad has been featured as a keynote speaker in the world's largest expos and conferences, and has been on radio, television, and various internet programs. His work has been published in several leading magazines, including *Whole Self Times, Sedona Journal,* and *Yoga Journal,* as well as the cover feature in *Evolve* magazine. Michael Mirdad is respected as one of the finest and most diverse healers of our time and well-known for his ability to share the deepest teachings in a clear, applicable manner.